The Christian Symbols

Of the

Twelve Days of Christmas

The Christian Symbols
of the
Twelve Days of Christmas

As Presented by the St. Bede
Holy Mamas

ML Brei

MERIPOINT BOOKS

January 2023

Limited Printing.
Printed in the United States of America

MERIPOINT BOOKS

In Memory of

Katrina Michelle Prokop

d. February 3, 2020

A Holy Mama
who left us too soon

C ome to me, all ye who are weary and burdened and I will give you rest. Matt. 11:28

Table of Contents

Adoration of the Shepherds
1534

Lorenzo Lotto
Oil on Canvas
Brescia

Christmas begins

on the twenty-fifth of December. For many it also ends on the twenty-fifth. But it shouldn't because this day is traditionally the *first* day of the festive season of Christmastide also known as Twelvetide. It runs from December 25th to January 5th.

Most of us know about Christmastide through the English carol, *The Twelve Days of Christmas* which sings of a True Love who gives gifts to His Love for twelve days. Every Christmas, we sing the carol with spirit and speed, hoping not to forget the words.

We sing of each day when the True Love gives his gifts. On the first day he gives a partridge in a pear tree. On the second, he gives two turtle doves and a partridge in a pear tree. On the third day, he gives three French hens, two turtle doves, and a partridge in a pear tree. And so it goes; every day True Love gives new gifts in addition to all of the gifts he gave the previous day. By the twelfth day, the recipient has received 12 partridges, 22 turtle doves, 30 French hens, 36 calling birds, 40 gold rings, 42 geese a-laying, 42 swans a-swimming, 40 maids a-milking, 36 ladies dancing, 30 lords a-leaping, 22 pipers piping, and twelve drummers drumming. Mathematically speaking, this is recursive gift-giving. Practically speaking, it is too much.

A question springs to mind when singing this carol: Why are we singing this? The lyrics are ridiculous. Most of the gifts are birds or people, not the usual things one would give. Why these gifts?

Well, this carol has been around for a long time. It was set to music and the words were standardized in 1909, after which it became extremely popular. Long before it became a carol, however, it was published in the English children's book *Mirth without Mischief* in 1780. It was a memory game played on Twelfth Night. But even before that, variants of the verse were known in Ireland, Scotland, and across the Channel in France.

Some believe it was initially composed during those years in England when Catholicism was outlawed. These were the dangerous years after the Dissolution of the Monasteries and other reform movements swept across the British Isles. These were the years during which at one point Christmas itself was banned, because it was considered too Catholic. These were years of grave secrecy for Catholics: secret places, secret sacraments, and secret messages encoded in letters, children's rhymes and everywhere. Could it be that *The Twelve Days of Christmas* also held secrets that only those with the key could decipher?

Nobody knows for certain.

We're left with puzzling lyrics from long ago, altered here and there, without the original key.

Yet, surprisingly, today we have a Christian interpretation of the lyrics - the author of which is another mystery. This interpretation gives us symbolic meanings for each of the gifts that correspond to basic tenants of Christianity. It is a form of catechism for those of Christian faith: a fun way to memorize what we believe is true. This catechismal key is explained in the next section.

The Twelve Days of Christmas are meant to be twelve days of joy and celebration. It represents the journey of the Three Kings in search of the Christ Child. The season ends when their journey ends, the night before Epiphany or Three Kings Day.

This season has been celebrated for over 1400 years, having been established in 567 by the Council of Tours. By 878, King Alfred the Great had instituted a law allowing most Britains to abstain from work during Christmastide. It became a time of feasting, almsgiving, and gift giving. In the present age, in our bustling lives, we have mostly forgotten these ancient roots.

I believe it is possible to bring the joy and meaning of Christmastide back into our lives. We start at the beginning.

On the first day of Christmas, My True Love gives to me, a partridge in a pear tree. The "partridge in a pear tree" represents Jesus who voluntarily dies to protect His own. "My True Love" is God the Father who gives us the greatest gift of all, His Son, Jesus. We know how to celebrate this day, the Feast day of the Nativity of Our Lord. We do it every year by celebrating God's great gift to us. We exchange gifts in commemoration of His gift and we worship the newborn Jesus.

4

And the remaining days of Christmastide? There are many ways to celebrate. First, we can keep Christmas decorations displayed, especially our nativity scenes with all figures present except the Three Wisemen and their camels who are still en route.

The next eleven days may be celebrated by following centuries-old traditions: exchanging small gifts, giving to the poor, participating in feast days, attending services, and visiting friends and neighbors.

If we think about Christmastide with respect to *The Twelve Days of Christmas*, it is a perfect time to do kind things for others bearing in mind the Christian symbolism of the gifts of each day.

This is what the Holy Mamas of St. Bede did for me during Christmastide 2021. I had to begin a new life-saving medication, one which would cause severe side-effects. The Holy Mamas knew how difficult it would be for me. They banded together and using the spiritual meanings of the gifts in *The Twelve Days of Christmas* as inspiration, they presented me with acts of kindness and small gifts for twelve days. They called it the *Twelve Days of Christmas Recovery Rally*.

Their acts of kindness brought tremendous joy into my life. And I hope that by sharing with you the keys to the Christian interpretation of the Twelve Days, you, too, will find joy.

Now, turn the page, view the gifts that magically appeared during my Christmastide 2021, think about the meanings behind the gifts, the "code" of the *Twelve Days of Christmas.* Consider also the various ideas for celebrating each day.

Finally once you have finished the carol, you will find a guide for creating your own special Christmastide!

I BELIEVE

Welcome to your "12 Days of Christmas Recovery Rally"! Every day from now until January 5th a Holy Mama will be visiting you or sending you (via e-mail) well wishes for health.

NORTH POLE SPECIAL DELIVERY

On the First Day of Christmas

The Holy Mamas gave to me:

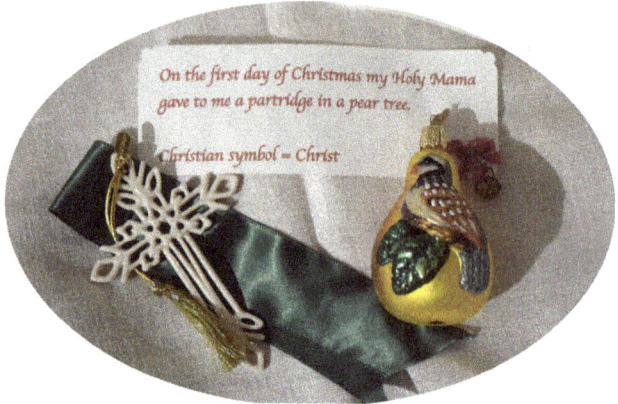

On the first day of Christmas my Holy Mama gave to me a partridge in a pear tree.

Christian symbol = Christ

A partridge in a pear tree.

A Partridge Glass Ornament
a Lenox Cross

Christ, Salvation

First Day, December 25

Feast Day of the Nativity of Our Lord Jesus Christ

For God so loved the world that He gave his only Son, that everyone who believes in Him might not perish but have everlasting life. (John 3:16)

The partridge will sacrifice its life to protect its young. The partridge represents **Jesus Christ,** who protects us from the snares of the devil. He gave Himself as the ultimate sacrifice.

The pear tree represents Jesus, the **salvation of mankind**, in contrast to the apple tree which symbolizes the fall of Adam and Eve.

> And there is salvation in no one else, for there is no other name under heaven given among men by which we must be saved.(Acts 4:12)

We celebrate the birth of Jesus Christ by attending Mass, exchanging gifts, and feasting.

A Partridge in a Pear Tree
2022

In the style of Giotto
Generated by ML + DALL-E 2
OpenAI

The Nativity
1523

Lorenzo Lotto, 1480-1556
Venice
Oil on panel
National Gallery of Art

On the Second Day of Christmas

The Holy Mamas gave to me:

Two Turtle Doves

A Pair of Dove Earrings

The Old and New Testaments

Second Day, December 26

The two turtle doves symbolize the **Old and New Testaments** of the bible which contain the story of the Christian faith and God's plan for the world.

Two turtle doves also call to mind the doves offered as a sacrifice when Jesus was presented in the temple:

they brought Him to Jerusalem to present Him to the Lord … and to offer a sacrifice according to what is said in the law of the Lord, a pair of turtledoves or two young pigeons. (Luke 2:22-24)

As celebrated in the carol *Good King Wenceslas*, today is St. Stephen's Day (first martyr, AD 36).

Stephen, a man full of God's grace and power, performed great wonders and signs among the people. (Acts 6:8)

According to legend, Jesus miraculously healed St. Stephen's ailing horse. In Europe, this is the day horses and oats are blessed, bread in the shape of horseshoes is eaten, and horse parades and festivals are held.

This is Boxing Day in Great Britain, traditionally when money and food are distributed to workers and the poor.

A Prayer to St. Stephen

O Glorious St. Stephen, first of the martyrs,
for the sake of christ you gave up your life
in testimony of the truth of His divine teaching.

Obtain for us, dear St. Stephen,
the faith, the hope, the love and the courage of martyrs.

When we are tempted to shirk our duty, or deny our
faith, come to our assistance as a shining example of the
courage of martyrs, and win for us a love like your own.

We ask it of you for the honor of Jesus Christ,
our Lord who is model and reward of all martyrs.
Amen.

Two Turtle Doves
2022

In the style of Giotto
Generated by ML + DALL-E 2
OpenAI

Saint Stephen in Glory
1601

Giacomo Cavedone 1577-1660
Italian Baroque Painter, Bolognese School

Galleria Estense, Modena

On the Third Day of Christmas

The Holy Mamas gave to me:

Three French Hens

Three Mint Chocolates (sugarfree!)

Faith, Hope, and Love
1 Corinthians 13:13

Third Day, December 27

And now these three remain: faith, hope, and love. But the greatest of these is love. (1 Corinthians 13:13)

Three French hens, known for their beauty and rarity, represent the virtues **faith, hope, and love.**

We celebrate the Feast Day of St. John the Evangelist today. He is the only disciple who did not die a martyr's death.

> The Word was made flesh and dwelt upon us.
> (John 1:14)

According to legend, St. John once drank a cup of poisoned wine and did not get ill. Therefore, in areas of Europe, wine and cider are brought to church for blessing. Some of the blessed wine is drunk that night, the rest is carefully stored as a sacramental. It is then drunk on important occasions such as a wedding, the birth of a child, the beginning of a trip, or a grave illness.

Three French Hens in a Flower Garden
2022

In the style of Vermeer
Generated by ML + DALL-E 2
OpenAI

Print of John, The Evangelist
1 January 1550

Crispijn von Passe de Oude
1564-1637, Utrecht
Dutch Publisher and Engraver

Ghent University Library

On the Fourth Day of Christmas

The Holy Mamas gave to me:

Four Calling Birds

Holiday Soap and Lotion
Decorated with four birds

*The four Evangelists: Matthew,
Mark, Luke, and John*

Fourth Day, December 28

The four calling birds represent the four gospel writers (**evangelists**):

St. Matthew

St. Mark　　　St. Luke　　　St. John

Today is Childermas, the feast day of the Holy Innocents of Bethlehem slaughtered by King Herod.

> Then Herod, when he saw that he had been tricked by the wise men … sent and killed all the male children in Bethlehem…who were two years old or under, according to the time which he had ascertained from the wise men. (Matt. 2:16)

On this day, babies and young children are blessed either at Mass by the priest or at home by a parent.

Young children or "innocents" are served a special porridge called *Holy Innocents' Pabulum* made of cream of wheat, milk, sugar, and cinnamon.

In Spain, in recognition of the Magis' "trick" on Herod, everyone is allowed to play practical jokes on each other.

A Renaissance Oil Painting of Four
Calling Birds in a Tree
January 2, 2023

Generated by ML + DALL-E 2
OpenAI

The Symbols of the Four Evangelists

St. Mark — a winged lion
St Matthew — a divine man
St. Luke — a winged ox
St. John — a rising eagle

The Four Evangelists
820 AD

Aachen Gospel Folio 13r
A Carologian depiction
Aachen Cathedral Treasury

On the Fifth Day of Christmas

The Holy Mamas gave to me:

Five Golden Rings

Five Beautiful Carolers delivering a Basket
of White Candles and an Assignment to
read passages of light from

The Pentateuch

Fifth Day: December 29

Genesis   Exodus
Leviticus   Numbers   Deuteronomy

Five golden rings (the rings around the necks of the ring-necked pheasant) symbolize the first five books of the bible known as the Pentateuch.

The following passages in the Pentateuch show us the light of our faith:

Genesis 1:1-5
Exodus 3:1 6
Leviticus 24:1-4
Numbers 9:15-18
Deuteronomy 5:1-33

A Renaissance Oil Painting of Five White
Candles in Silver Candelabra and Five
Books on a Table
January 2, 2023

Generated by ML + DALL·E 2
OpenAI

Pentateuch Scroll
ca 1225 AD

Written by Israel ben Isaac Ben Israel
Toledo, Spain
Animal Skin

On the Sixth Day of Christmas
The Holy Mamas gave to me:

Six Geese-a-laying

Beekman 1802 Milk Jug filled with
healing gifts

The Six Days of Creation

Sixth Day: December 30

God looked at everything he had made, and he found it very good. (Gen.1:31)

The six geese a-laying symbolize the six **days of creation** as "hatched" by God:

Day 1: God created the heavens and the earth.
Day 2: God created the sky and seas.
Day 3: God created the land and plants.
Day 4: God created the sun, moon, and stars.
Day 5: God created fish and birds.
Day 6: God created land animals and man.

On the seventh day, God rested.

Today is the Feast Day of the Holy Family. In commemoration, we write *JMJ* (Jesus, Mary, Joseph) at the bottom of our correspondence.

JMJ

For the Lord sets a father in honor over his children and confirms a mother's authority over her sons. Those who honor their father, atone for their sins; they store up riches who respect their mother. Those who honor their father will have joy in their own children, and when they pray they are heard. Those who respect their father will live a long life; those who obey the Lord honor their mother.

(Sir 3:2-6, 12-14)

JMJ

The Heavenly and Earthly Trinities
The Pedroso Murillo
ca 1675-1682

Bartolomé Esteban Murillo
Oil on canvas, Cádiz, Spain
National Gallery, London

On the Seventh Day of Christmas

The Holy Mamas gave to me:

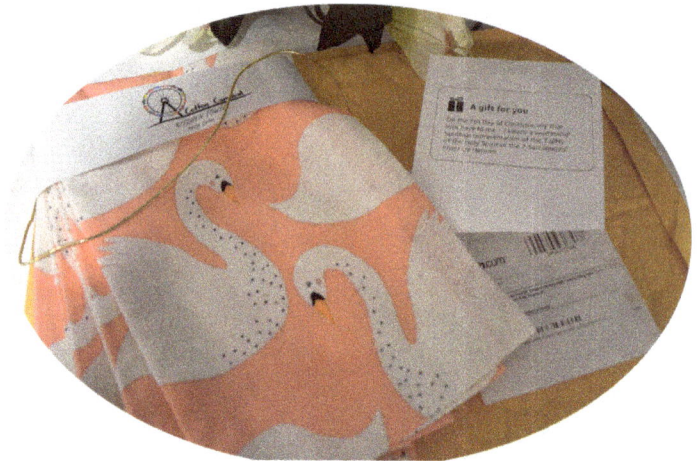

Seven Swans a Swimming

Swimming Swans on Tea Towels

The Seven Gifts of the Holy Spirit or Seven Sacraments

Seventh Day: December 31

We have different gifts, according to the grace given us. (Rom. 12:6)

The seven swans a-swimming symbolize the seven

Gifts of the Holy Spirit:

prophesy

ministry   teaching

exhortation   giving   leading   compassion

Seven is the number of perfection in Judaism. And seven swans swimming gracefully through peaceful waters give us a symbolic glimpse of perfection in heaven.

This is the feast day of St. Sylvester, who was pope from 314-335. He died on December 31st. According to legend, he healed Emperor Constantine of leprosy and thereby converted him.

This evening, New Year's Eve, is celebrated as Silvester night (Silvesternacht) in areas in Europe with all of the fireworks, feasting, and festivities of New Year's Eve.

Prayer to St. Sylvester

Come, O Lord, to the help of your people,
Sustained by the intercession of Pope Saint Sylvester,
so that, running the course of this present life under
your guidance, we may happily attain life without end.
Through our Lord Jesus Christ, your Son, Who lives and reigns
with you in the unity of the Holy Spirit one God,
for ever and ever.
Amen.

Coronation of Constantine with Pope Sylvester
Ca. 1247

Unknown artist
San Silvestro Chapel
Santi Quattro Coronati, Rome

On the Eighth Day of Christmas
The Holy Mamas gave to me:

Eight Maids-a-milking

Faith-Hope-Peace Hand Towel & Soap

The Eight Beatitudes

Eighth Day: January 1

The Solemnity of Mary, Mother of God
Holy Day of Obligation

On the eighth day, …, He was named Jesus, the name the angel had given Him before He was conceived. (Luke 2:21)

The eight maids a-milking are the **eight beatitudes**:

> "Blessed are the the poor in spirit, …
> Blessed are those who mourn, …
> Blessed are the meek, …
> Blessed are those who hunger and thirst
> for righteousness, …
> Blessed are the merciful, …
> Blessed are the pure in heart, …
> Blessed are the peacemakers, …
> Blessed are those who are persecuted
> for righteousness' sake,
> for theirs is the kingdom of heaven."
>
> (Matthew 5:3-10)

Milkmaids are humble servants who exemplify the qualities of these beatitudes.

This day is dedicated to Mary, Mother of God and her self-less love. She is honored as Queen of Peace in concordance with World Day of Peace.

Madonna and Child Triptych
a. 1370

Annunciation, Visitation, Nativity, Mary sleeps while St. Joseph holds Jesus, Adoration of Magi, Presentation in the temple

Ivory
French
Louvre Museum

Photo by Marie-Lan Nguyen

A nd seeing the multitudes, he went up into a mountain: and when he was seated, his disciples came to him. Then he began to speak. (Matt 5:1-2)

Sermon on the Mount
1877

Carl Bloch
Oil on Copper
Denmark

On the Ninth Day of Christmas

The Holy Mamas gave to me:

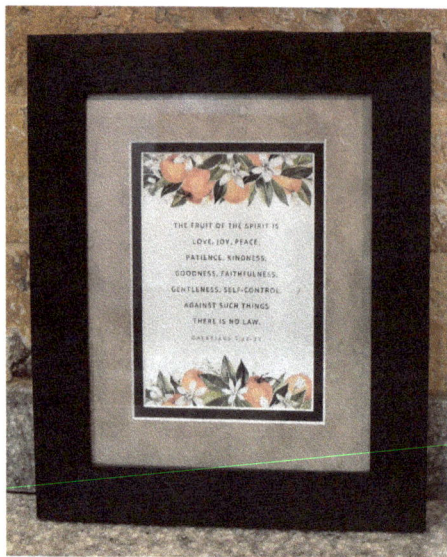

THE FRUIT OF THE SPIRIT IS
LOVE, JOY, PEACE,
PATIENCE, KINDNESS,
GOODNESS, FAITHFULNESS,
GENTLENESS, SELF-CONTROL.
AGAINST SUCH THINGS
THERE IS NO LAW.
GALATIANS 5:22-23

Nine Ladies Dancing

A Framed Print

The nine Fruits of the Holy Spirit

Ninth Day: January 2

B ut the fruit of the Spirit is **love, joy, peace, patience, kindness, goodness, faithfulness, gentleness, self-control**

Against such things there is no law.
(Galatians 5:22-23)

The nine ladies dancing are the nine **fruits of the Holy Spirit.**

The nine ladies dancing also represent the

Nine choirs of Angels

Seraphim, Cherubim, Thrones
Dominions, Virtues, Powers
Principalities, Archangel, Angel

The Choirs of Angels
ca. 1150

Hildegard von Bingen
Scivias I.6
From the Rupertsberg Manuscript folio 38r.

Fruit of the Holy Spirit
1870

John Hardman Powell, cartoonist
Stained Glass Window

Christ Church Cathedral, Dublin, Ireland

Photo by Andreas F. Borchert

On the Tenth Day of Christmas

The Holy Mamas gave to me:

Ten Lords a-leaping

A gift certificate to Lord & Taylor

The Ten Commandments

Tenth Day: January 3

The ten lords a-leaping are the judges of the land and represent:

The
Ten Commandments

1. "I am the Lord thy God, thou shalt not have any gods before Me.

2. Thou shalt not take the name of the Lord in vain.

3. Remember to keep holy the Sabbath day.

4. Honor thy father and mother.

5. Thou shalt not kill.

6. Thou shalt not commit adultery.

7. Thou shalt not steal.

8. Thou shalt not bear false witness against thy neighbor.

9. Thou shalt not covet thy neighbor's wife.

10. Thou shalt not covet thy neighbor's goods."

(The Decalogue, Deuteronomy 5:6)

This is also the Feast day of the Holy Name of Jesus.

S he will bear a son, and you shall call his name Jesus, for he will save his people from their sins. All this took place to fulfill what the Lord had spoken by the prophet:

> "Behold, the virgin shall conceive and bear a son, and they shall call his name Immanuel." (Matthew 1:21-23)

The Adoration of the Holy Name of Jesus
1577-1579

El Greco
Oil on Canvas
El Escorial, Spain

Moses
ca. 1408-10

Lorenzo Monaco
Tempera on wood, gold ground
Florence, Italy

Metropolitan Museum of Art

On the Eleventh Day of Christmas

The Holy Mamas gave to me:

Eleven Pipers Piping

Eleven Beautiful carolers singing hymns
A collection of Eleven Teas

The Eleven faithful disciples

Eleventh Day: January 4

To the Jews who had believed him, Jesus said, "If you hold to my teaching, you are really my disciples. Then you will know the truth, and the truth will set you free." (John 8:31)

The eleven pipers piping are the eleven **faithful disciples** at the time of resurrection and ascension.

Simon (Peter)
Andrew
James
John
Philip
Bartholomew
Matthew
Thomas
James, son of Alphaeus
Simon, who was called the Zealot
Judas, son of Jam

(Judas Iscariot, the twelfth, betrayed Jesus)

But the Lord is faithful, and he will strengthen you and protect you from the evil one. (Thess. 3:3)

Christ Taking Leave of the Apostles
ca. 1308-11

Duccio di Buoninsegna
Altarpiece, Tempera on wood
Siena, Italy

Museo dell'Opera del Duomo, Siena

On the Twelfth Day of Christmas

The Holy Mamas gave to me:

Twelve Drummers drumming

12 Long-stemmed Yellow Roses
A Planner for my days
A Healing Mass

*The 12 points of belief in
the Apostle's Creed*

Twelfth Day: January 5

The twelve drummers drumming are the 12 points of belief in the **Apostles' Creed** (the structure of the first part of the catechism):

1. I believe in God, the Father almighty, Creator of Heaven and Earth.
2. And in Jesus Christ, his only Son, our Lord
3. Who was conceived by the power of the Holy Spirit and born of the Virgin Mary
4. He suffered under Pontius Pilate, was crucified, died, and was buried.
5. He descended into hell. On the third day, he rose again.
6. He ascended into heaven and is seated at the right hand of the Father.
7. He will come again to judge the living and the dead.
8. I believe in the Holy Spirit,
9. the holy Catholic Church, the Communion of Saints,
10. the forgiveness of sins,
11. the resurrection of the body,
12. and life everlasting.

This evening is Twelfth Night when celebrations are held, Shakespeare's play, *Twelfth Night*, is performed, and at the end of it all, decorations are taken down. The three Wise Men have reached their destination.

They were overjoyed at seeing the star.

(Matt. 2:10)

The Journey of the Magi
ca. 1433-35

Sassetta (Stephano di Giovanni)
Fragment from small Altarpiece
Tempera on gold, wood
Siena, Italy

Metropolitan Museum of Art

Annunciation to the Shepherds
ca. 1460

Sassetta (Stephano di Giovanni)
Leaf from a Book of Hours
Ink, Tempera, and gold on vellum
Troyes, France

Cleveland Museum of Art

Create Your Christmastide Celebration

◆ *With acts of kindness towards others* ◆

Is there someone you know who is particularly sad, or recovering from an illness, or about to face a difficult situation? Perhaps you feel deeply for this person, but you don't know how to help.

If you present this person with a special Christmastide (as the Holy Mamas did for me) then you will be doing a Great Act of Kindness.

It doesn't take much to do this. The gifts or acts should be within your means. They can be as simple as a cheerful email each day, symbolically sending "a partridge in a pear tree," etc. You saw how imaginative the Holy Mamas were in cheering me up. You can do the same. On the next pages there is a chart to fill out. Use this to organize your ideas. You might share it with others to join you in this endeavor. Following the chart are blank pages for capturing more thoughts. Be creative; have fun! Unleash your compassion!

Christmastide Acts of Kindness

Day/ Date	Symbol	Gift Ideas
Day 1 **Dec 25**	Partridge/Pear Tree = Christ, Salvation	
Day 2 **Dec 26**	2 turtle doves = Old & New Testaments	
Day 3 **Dec 27**	3 French hens = Faith, Hope, & Love	
Day 4 **Dec 28**	4 calling birds = Sts Matthew, Mark, Luke, John	
Day 5 **Dec 29**	5 golden rings = Pentateuch, first 5 books of the Bible	
Day 6 **Dec 30**	6 geese-a-laying = Days of Creation	

Day/Date	Symbol	Gift Ideas
Day 7 **Dec 31**	7 Swans-a-swimming = Gifts of the Holy Spirit	
Day 8 **Jan 1**	8 maids a-milking = The 8 Beatitudes	
Day 9 **Jan 2**	9 ladies dancing = 9 Fruits of the Holy Spirit	
Day 10 **Jan 3**	10 lords-a-leaping = 10 Commandments	
Day 11 **Jan 4**	11 pipers piping = 11 Faithful Disciples	
Day 12 **Jan 5**	12 drummers = 12 points of belief of The Apostle's Creed	

Christmastide Feast Days

Day/Date	Feast
Day 1 Dec 25	Nativity of our Lord Jesus Christ
Day 2 Dec 26	St. Stephen'sDay
Day 3 Dec 27	Feast of St. John
Day 4 Dec 28	Childermas
Day 5 Dec 29	
Day 6 Dec 30	Feast Day Holy Family
Day 7 Dec 31	Sylvester Night /New Year's Eve
Dec 8 Jan 1	Solemnity of Mary
Day 9 Jan 2	
Day 10 Jan 3	Feast of the Holy Name of Jesus
Day 11 Jan 4	
Day 12 Jan 5	Eve of Epiphany; Twelfthnight

Notes

You are my refuge and shield. I have put my hope in your word. (Psalm 119:11:4)

✝

Acknowledgements

I wish to thank the wonderful Holy Mamas of St. Bede who made my Christmastide 2021-22 joyful. Special thanks to Heather Clemens, Gwen Sturdy, Elizabeth Berquist, Liz Hanson, Becky Carvajal, Kathy Gillespie, Jennifer Gillette, and the Berquist Family Carolers.

I also thank Ellen Hooper, my loving sister-in-law, for her encouragement and suggestions for this guide.

The twelve yellow roses are for friendship.

The Adoration of the Magi
c. 1466

Nikolaus Obilman (1435-1488)
National Museum of Warsaw

When Jesus was born

In Bethlehem, in the days of King Herod,
Behold, magi from the east arrived in
Jerusalem,
Saying, "where is the newborn King of the
Jews? We saw His star at its rising and have
come to do Him homage."
. . . And behold, the star that they had seen at
its rising preceded them, until it came and
stopped over the place where the Child was.
They were overjoyed at seeing the star,
And on entering the house they saw the Child
with Mary His mother. They prostrated
themselves and did Him homage.
Then they opened their treasures and offered
Him gifts of gold, frankincense, and myrrh.

(Matthew 2:1-2, 9-11)